Little Book of Answers

Where Is The Astronaut?

Written by Michele Ashley

Space

Vital Vocabulary

Earth 14

Hubble telescope 8

moon
12

space
6

spacecraft
4

space station
10

In the spacecraft.

spacecraft

In space.

space

At the Hubble telescope.

Hubble telescope

Outside the space station.

space station

On the moon.

On Earth.

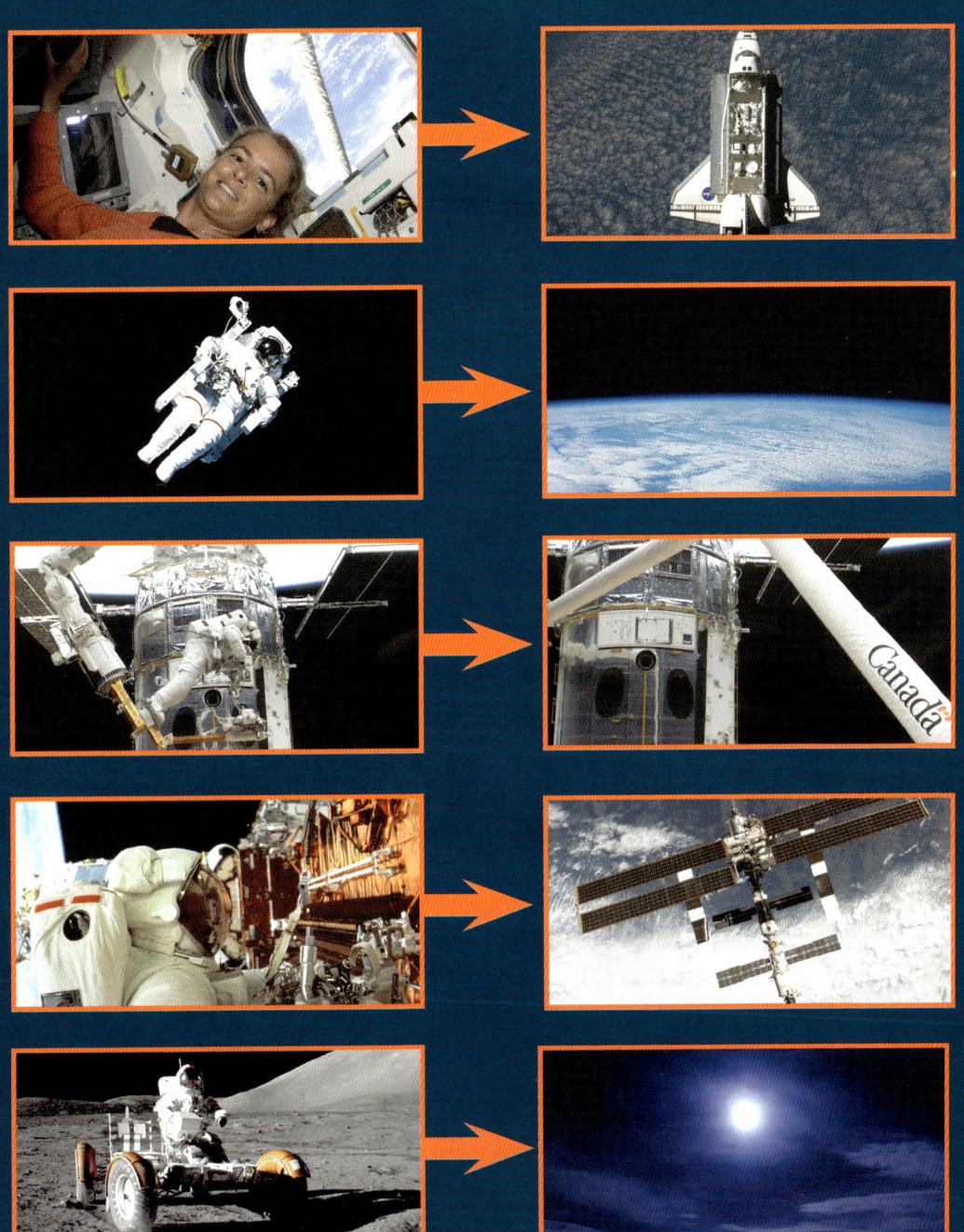

Critical Thinking

Where is this astronaut?
What do you think he is doing?